Easy Piano

SOLO: A STAR WARS STORY
MUSIC FROM THE MOTION PICTURE SOUNDTRACK

HAN SOLO THEME AND ORIGINAL STAR WARS MUSIC BY **JOHN WILLIAMS**
SCORE COMPOSED AND ADAPTED BY **JOHN POWELL**

ISBN: 978-1-5400-3270-6

HAL•LEONARD®

Visit Hal Leonard Online at
www.halleonard.com

Contact Us:
Hal Leonard
7777 West Bluemound Road
Milwaukee, WI 53213
Email: info@halleonard.com

In Europe contact:
Hal Leonard Europe Limited
Distribution Centre, Newmarket Road
Bury St Edmunds, Suffolk, IP33 3YB
Email: info@halleonardeurope.com

In Australia contact:
Hal Leonard Australia Pty. Ltd.
4 Lentara Court
Cheltenham, Victoria, 3192 Australia
Email: info@halleonard.com.au

THE ADVENTURES OF HAN

Composed by
JOHN WILLIAMS

Moderately fast

MEET HAN

Composed by JOHN POWELL
and JOHN WILLIAMS

decresc.

CORELLIA CHASE

Composed by JOHN POWELL
and JOHN WILLIAMS

Moderately fast

TRAIN HEIST

Composed by
JOHN POWELL

Moderately slow

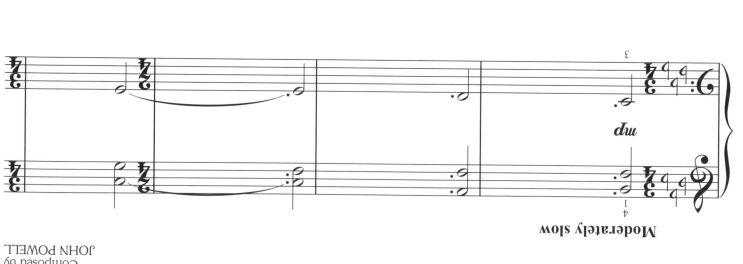

CHICKEN IN THE POT

Composed by
JOHN POWELL

Slow Funk

THE GOOD GUY

Composed by
JOHN POWELL

Slowly, very freely

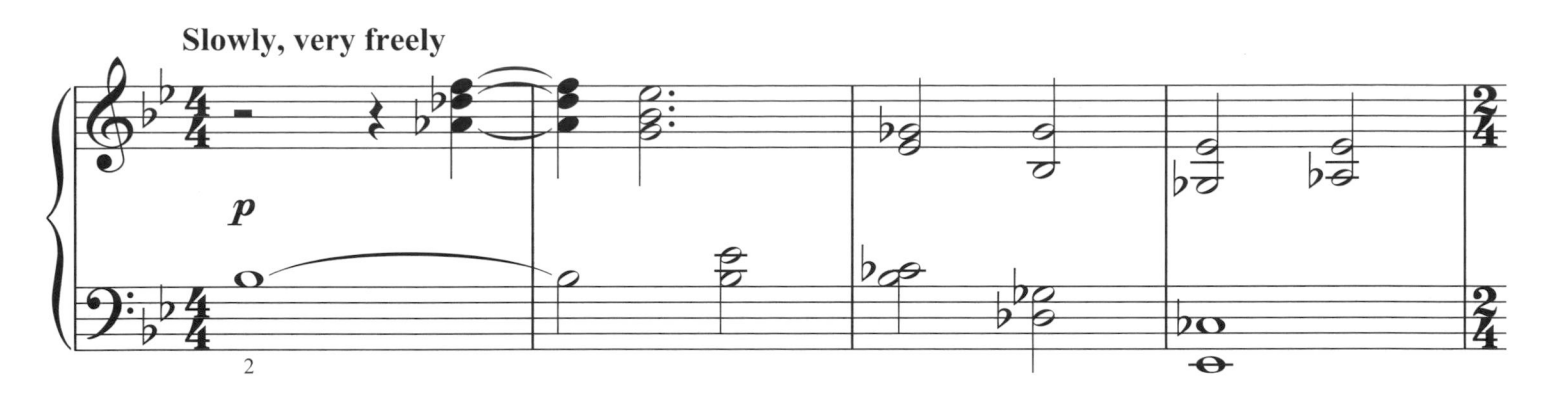

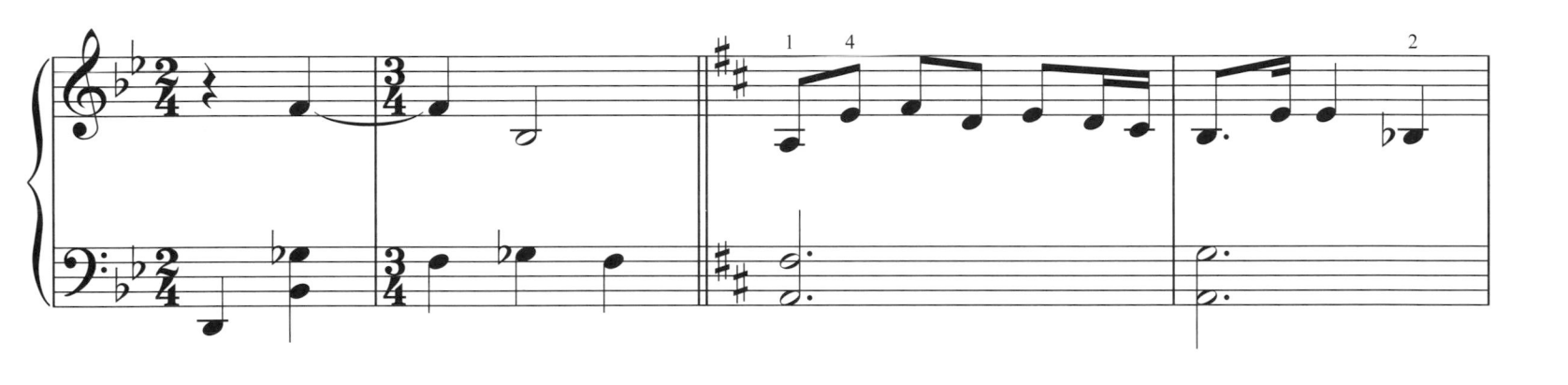

Moderately slow, expressively

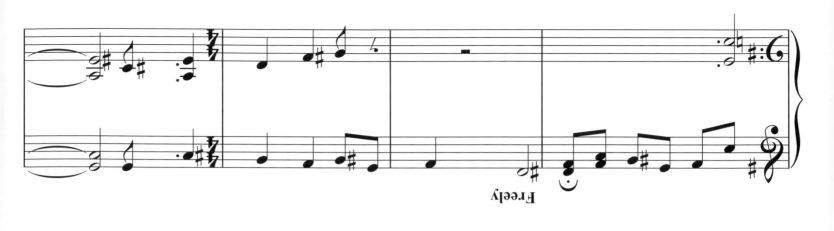

LANDO'S CLOSET

Composed by
JOHN POWELL

Moderately slow, expressively

MINE MISSION

Composed by JOHN POWELL
and JOHN WILLIAMS

SAVAREEN STAND-OFF

Composed by JOHN POWELL
and JOHN WILLIAMS

Slowly, expressively

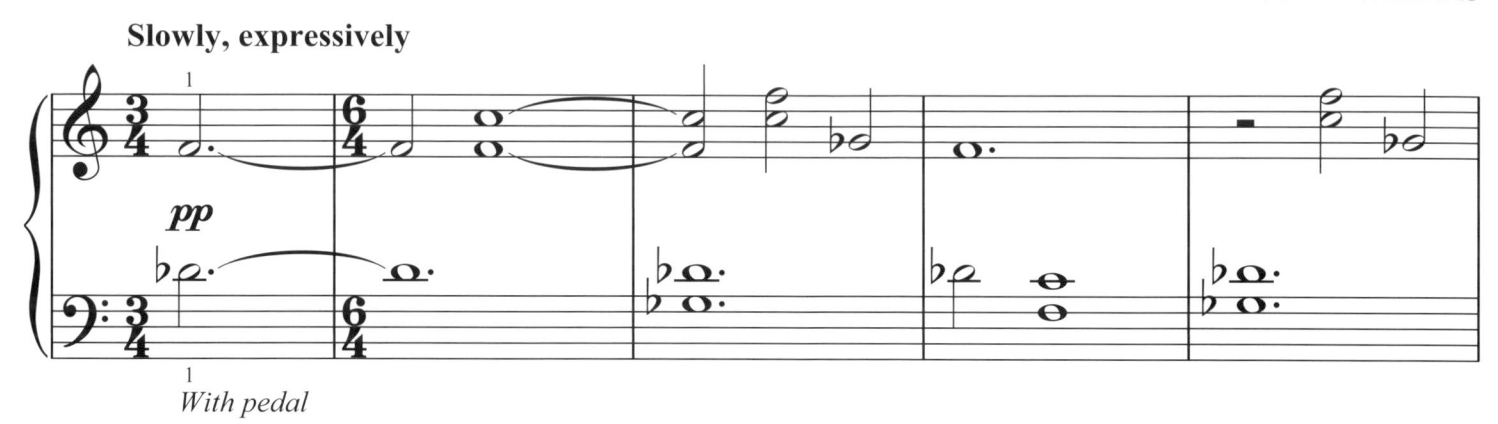

With pedal

More steadily

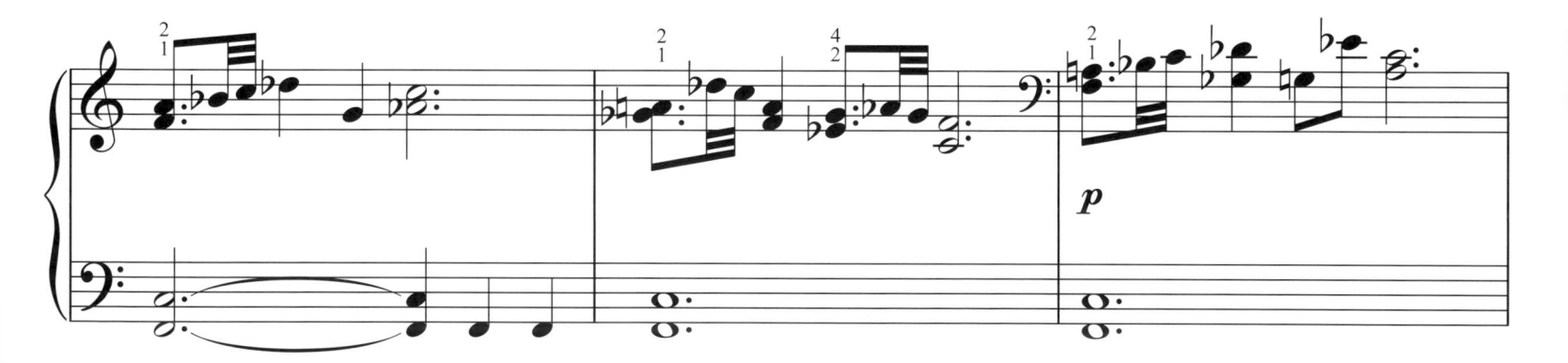

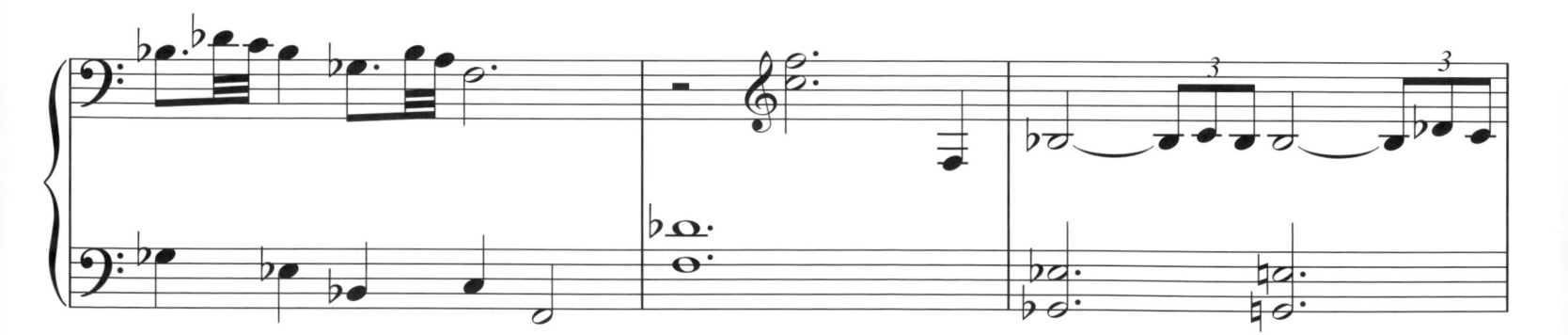